THE NIGHT BEFORE SERIES™

The Night Before Noah Rode on the Ark

Written by: Timothy Penland
Illustrated by: Mary Alice Ramsey

canecreekpublishers

dawson media®

'Twas the night before Noah
Rode on the ark
He loaded the boat
And now it was dark.

It was already raining
The skies were pitch black
God had just closed the door
Noah wouldn't look back.

He thought for a moment
How this came to pass
A message from God,
A very big task.

His friends had all laughed.
They thought he was crazy.
It never had rained!
It'd hardly been hazy!

But Noah just said,
"One day you will see.
God told me to do it!
You'll wish you were me!"

God spoke to Noah
About building this boat
He gave clear instructions
So it really would float.

Noah worked on this big ship
A very long time
Using God's details
He followed each line.

The ark was a refuge
A place he could stay
To weather the storm
God had promised today.

Noah gathered his family
They helped build the boat
And filled it with livestock
From rhinos to goats.

There were at least two
Of each kind of beast
From the north and the south
And the west and the east.

Big ones and small ones
Fat ones and thin
All came to the ark
And all were let in.

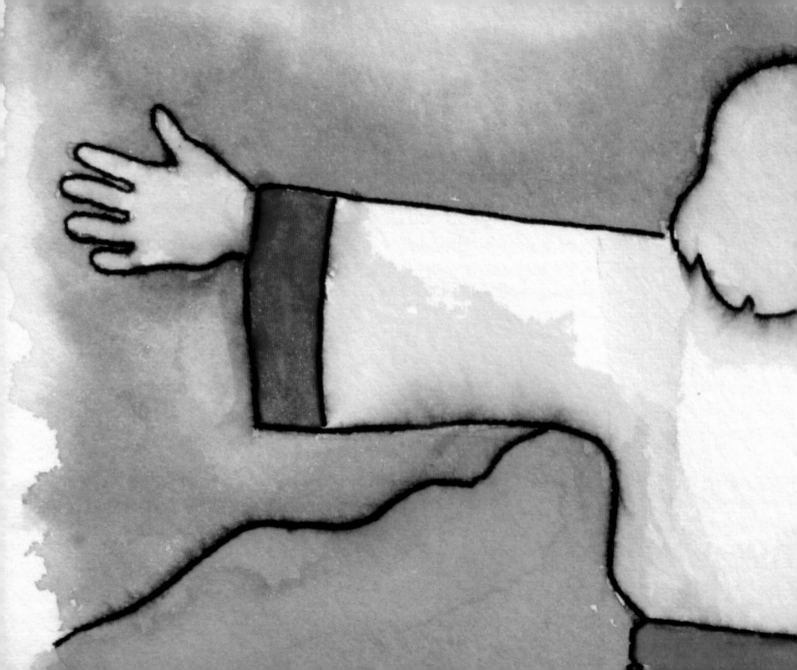

So why build a boat,
this big and this wide?
It didn't make sense,
to climb in and hide.

"Men just don't listen
Except for one man.
I'll start things all over,"
God said of His plan.

To cover the earth,
All of the land
With water from rain
'Til no one could stand.

It rained and it rained,
day after day.
Noah just didn't know,
how long it would stay.

Noah let go a raven,
it was strong, big and black,
to look for a sign
but it never came back.

Then finally one morning
The sun came out bright
It had been many days
But the end was in sight.

He let out a dove,
it was small and quite weak.
It soon came right back,
with a leaf in its beak.

Noah now knew the truth
He could open the ark
The earth was renewed!
It looked like a park!

Up in the sky
There was a grand sight
Something amazing
The colors were bright.

Noah wondered out loud
"Why is it there?"
"Why put such an arch
Way up in the air?"

God said that he did it
So all men would know
"I am making a promise
The sign - a rainbow."

"It means the great flood,
Is a thing of the past
It won't happen again
The first and the last.

Noah prayed and thanked God
All day until dark
For keeping him safe
Right there in the ark.

This story reminds us
To always obey
Whatever God tells us
He'll show us the way.

Remember that Noah
Found out that he could
Trust God to protect him
In a boat made of wood.

Almost 30 years ago my wife and I labored to paint a depiction of Noah's story. It was designed to be used as a mural in the church we were attending. The paintings were done in memory of our son Timothy Matthew Penland who left us after barely 2 months of life. This book, which relates the very same story, is dedicated to his memory in hopes that it will bring joy into the lives of many families just as Matthew brought joy into our home.

Acknowledgements

Special thanks to Mary Alice Ramsey for her wonderful illustrations which has brought this story to life and to Terry for his support and encouragement. Special thanks also go to Kirk Hawkins for his creative and insightful work in getting the book ready to print. Thanks to Ben for his expertise and patience in working through all of the details required to put this work into the hands of children and their parents. As always I am enormously grateful to Joy, my wife, companion and best friend for almost as long as I can remember. Thanks seems inadequate to express my gratitude to our Maker/Creator/ Savior who is the source of this story.

Timothy Penland

© 2010 by Timothy Penland

Dawson Media and the Dawson Media logo are registered trademarks of NavPress. Absence of ® in connection with marks of Dawson Media or other parties does of indicate an absence of registration of those marks.

ISBN: 978-1-93565-104-8

Library of Congress Control Number: 2010923111

Illustrations by Mary Alice Ramsey
Cover and Interior Design by Kirk Hawkins

Printed in India

1 2 3 4 5 6 7 8 / 14 13 12 11 10